1

The Life and Adventures of Venture Smith And Poems By A Slave
PREPARED FOR PUBLICATION BY:
HISTORIC PUBLISHING

Slavery Books & African American History Resources
https://slaverybooks.blogspot.com

The Life and Adventures of Venture Smith
And
Poems By A Slave
(Annotated)
By
Joe Mitchell, MA

Writings
By
Venture Smith
&
George Moses Horton

Biography with Historical Context
By
Joe Mitchel

Other Historical Commentary
Contributions
By
Carter G. Woodson

CONTENTS

A Narrative of the Life and Adventures of Venture, a Native of Africa: But Resident above Sixty Years in the United States of America. Related by Himself. With Poems By A Slave

By
Venture Smith
&
George Moses Horton

Forward
By
J. Mitchell

Commentary Contributions
By
Carter G. Woodson

Biography with Historical Context

By

J. Mitchell

Information Regarding the Author Venture Smith and the Three Editions (1798, 1835, 1897) of His *Narrative.*

The Narrative of the Life of Venture Smith has been published three times. In 1835, the narrative was reprinted for the second time, and was Published by a *Descendant of Venture,* as it was originally; with only minor editorial changes incorporated. However, the third edition of the title was *Revised and Republished with Traditions by H. M. Selden, Haddam, Conn., in 1897.* It is to the benefit of the reader to know that all three editions are similarly titled: *A Narrative of the Life and Adventures of Venture, a Native of Africa: But Resident above Sixty Years in the United States of America. Related by Himself.* The third edition (1897), in addition to the aforementioned heading title also notes the following information on the title page: *New London: Printed in 1798. Reprinted A. D. 1835, and Published by a Descendant of Venture. Revised and Republished with Traditions by H. M. Selden, Haddam, Conn., 1897*[1].4

---

1 *This book is the first edition of three and was printed in 1798. The elements of differentiated interests in the third edition are the Traditions section added and edited by H.M. Selden. The purpose

of this explanation will continue below at the conclusion of this
brief biography section.

A BRIEF BIOGRAPHY OF THE AUTHOR VENTURE SMITH

Venture Smith was born in 1729 in Dukandarra, Guinea; and was the eldest son of a Guinea prince. When Smith was a young child, he and his family were captured and taken as prisoners by an invading army. Based on historical records, Venture Smith's father was killed by these invading kidnappers for refusing to comply with their staunch demands. Following his father's inhumane and heartless murder, Smith and his family were immediately taken captive by the invading army. When another army defeated his captors, Smith was sold to Robertson Mumford, and they departed to Anomabo and Barbados and then to Rhode Island. Ultimately, during twenty-six years of bondage, Smith would be sold three different times. Before buying his freedom in 1765 from his final owner, Col. Oliver Smith, from whom he took his surname. Ironically, after almost five years as master and slave, Oliver Smith and Venture Smith formed a mutual business partnership that remained intact for over three decades! By engaging in this business venture, the former slave master and slave effectively became equals in commerce. This relationship was a testament to Venture Smith's ingenuity and business shrewdness with a keen ability to capitalize on opportunistic business endeavors.

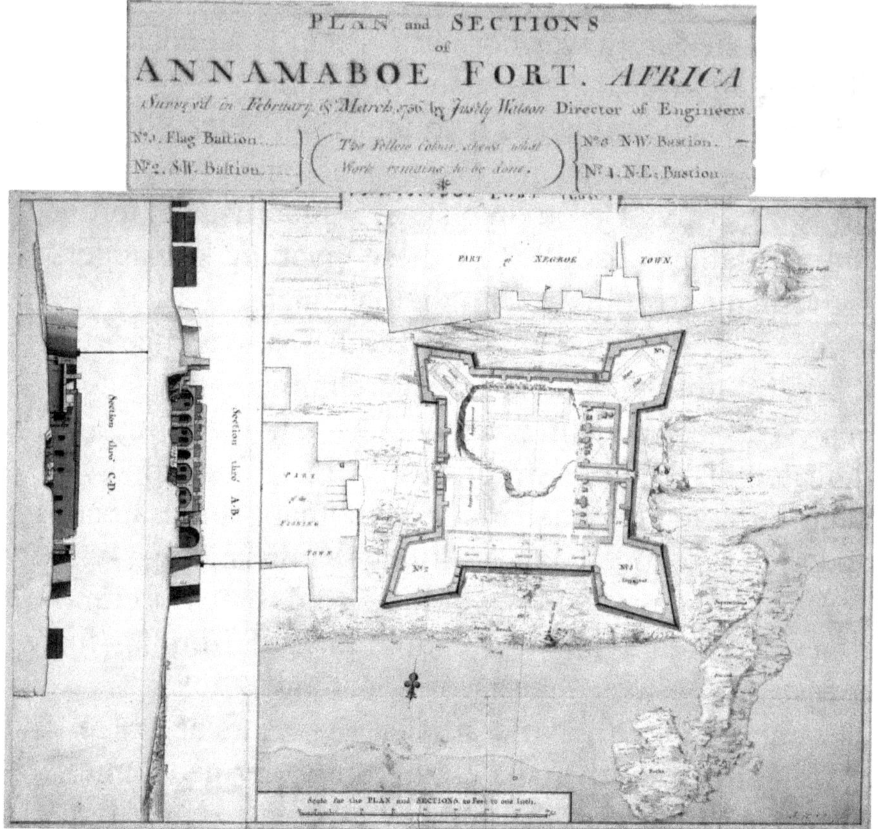

Annamaboe Fort, Ghana2

---

2 The images show the slave outpost at the time named **Annamaboe Fort,** Ghana where Venture Smith was purchased as a slave. Venture was held here in 1739. While under British control, approximately 5,000-7,000 African slaves per year were sold at Annamaboe Fort.

Smith grew up as a household slave on the Mumford plantation and married Meg (or Margaret), another one of Mumford's slaves, when he was 22 years of age. Shortly thereafter, on March 27, 1754 Venture escaped with two other slaves and one indentured servant, and then voluntarily returns approximately around the month of April, 1754. Smith and several of his fellow slaves attempted to escape, but their plans were abruptly aborted. Smith and his wife were then sold to Thomas Stanton. Smith vividly describes the conflicts he encountered with his new master's family. He goes on to describe how he eventually purchased freedom for his wife and two sons and one daughter by hiring himself out to others, doing odd jobs such as cutting wood, farming, and fishing. Meg and Venture Smith bore four children named Hannah, Solomon, Cuff, and Solomon. Three of the children were born enslaved, and the youngest son named Solomon (named after his older brother Solomon who died tragically at 16 while working on a whaling expedition) was born 1773 around the same time Meg's freedom was purchased. During the year of 1770, Venture purchased his two sons Solomon and Cuff for $200 each. Approximately three years later, in 1773 or 1774, he purchased his wife Meg for an undocumented amount. In 1775, the year America declared its independence from Britain, Venture Smith purchased his oldest child Hannah. Venture's son Cuff would later serve in the Continental Army 1781-1783.

FREE BLACK SLAVE OWNERS

To understand why freed slaves purchased other slaves it is necessary to analyze the work of the renowned African American historian Carter G. Woodson. Woodson was one of the first historians to have touched on black slave owners in his book titled: *Free Negro Owners of Slaves in the United States in 1830: Together with Absentee Ownership of Slaves in the United States in 1830.*[3] In his work, Woodson eloquently notes:

"The census records show that the majority of the Negro owners of slaves were such from the point of view of philanthropy. In many instances the husband purchased the wife or vice versa. The slaves belonging to such families were few compared with the large numbers found among the whites on the well-developed plantations. Slaves of Negroes were in some cases the children of a free father who had purchased his wife. If he did not thereafter emancipate the mother, as so many such husbands failed to do, his own children were born his slaves and were thus reported by the enumerators.

Some of these husbands were not anxious to liberate their wives immediately. They considered it advisable to put them on probation for a few years, and if they did not find them satisfactory, they would sell their

3 Woodson, Carter G., Free Negro Owners of Slaves in the United States in 1830: Together with Absentee Ownership of Slaves in the United States in 1830 (1924).

wives as other slaveholders disposed of Negroes. For example, a Negro shoemaker in Charleston, South Carolina, purchased his wife for $700; but on finding her hard to please, he sold her a few months thereafter for $750, gaining $50 by the transaction. The editor personally knew a man in Cumberland County, Virginia, whose mother was purchased by his father who had first bought himself. Becoming enamored of a man slave, she gave him her husband's manumission papers that they might escape together to free soil. Upon detecting this plot, the officers of the law received the impression that her husband had turned over the papers to the slave and arrested the freedman for the supposed offense. He had such difficulty in extricating himself from this complication that his attorney's fees amounted to $500. To pay them he disposed of his faithless wife for that amount.

Benevolent Negroes often purchased slaves to make their lot easier by granting them their freedom for a nominal sum, or by permitting them to work it out on liberal terms. John Barry Meachum, a Negro Baptist minister in St. Louis, thus came into possession of as many as twenty slaves by 1836. The exploitation type of Negro slaveholder, moreover, sometimes feeling the sting of conscience, liberated his slaves. Thus did Samuel Gibson, a Negro of Mississippi, in 1844, when he brought his six slaves to Cincinnati, Ohio, and settled them on free territory.

Having economic interests in common with the white slaveholders, the Negro owners of slaves often enjoyed the same social standing. It was not exceptional for them to attend the same church, to educate their children in the same private school, and to frequent the same places of amusement. Under such circumstances miscegenation easily followed. While those taking the census of 1830 did not generally record such facts, the few who did, as in the case of Nansemond County, Virginia, reported a situation which today would be considered alarming. In this particular County there appeared among the slaveholders free Negroes designated as Jacob of Read and white wife and Syphe of Matthews and white wife. Others reported with white wives were not slaveholders.

Practically all of these Negro slaveholders were in the South.

Slavery, however, at that time had not been exterminated altogether in the North, and even there the Negro was following in the footsteps of the white man, as this report will show."4

4 Woodson, Carter G., *Free Negro Owners of Slaves in the United States in 1830: Together with Absentee Ownership of Slaves in the United States in 1830.*

"FOLLOWING IN THE FOOTSTEPS OF WHITE MEN. . . ."[5]

Venture Smith was wise and industrious, and by purchasing his wife and family--he ultimately became a slaveholder for ***benevolent reasons,*** as previously described above by Woodson. Indeed, as concluded by Woodson, African Americans were *"following in the footsteps of white men."* From unfair business practices Smith discusses, to slavery, and lynching, blacks often engaged in the very behaviors they despised whites for practicing and endorsing. It is historical fact that African Americans lynched one another-although the motives were not usually based on racism.[6] Concerning black-on-black lynching and to further substantiate Woodson's aforementioned observations, *The Boston Independent* decorously affirmed in 1916 that, *"It is true that lynching is not confined to the Southern states, nor is it wholly a race evil, whites lynch whites and Negroes lynch Negroes, but this only proves it to be a contagious social disease, and the danger is in the contagiousness."*[7] The striking parallels found in Woodson work and Venture Smith's narrative give insights to how the system of slavery had variations, as did lynchings, and business dealings within the black

---

[5] Woodson, Carter G., *Free Negro Owners of Slaves in the United States in 1830: Together with Absentee Ownership of Slaves in the United States in 1830.*

[6] (a) Mitchell, Joe, *Forgotten Black-on-Black Lynching's in America. . . ., 1835-1935.*

(b) NAACP, *30 Years of Lynching In the United States: 1889-1918.*
Authored by National Association for the Advancement of Colored People

[7] The *Boston Independent*, February 7, 1916.

communities. Smith briefly touches on these subjects but does not go into detail. Therefore, to give the reader better historical context, these subject matters have been briefly explored in this section before the narrative begins.

VENTURE SMITH'S STORY CONTINUES

After purchasing his family's freedom, Venture Smith eventually saved enough of his earning to purchase property in East Haddam, New York. Smith was ambitious and did not stop there, he continued to amass and cultivate adjacent properties. Eventually, Smith was able to acquire over one hundred acres, and three different houses—astonishing feats, especially when considering his circumstances.

In 1798, when he was 69, Venture Smith most likely dictated his biographical narrative to Elisha Niles. Niles was a Connecticut schoolmaster. Throughout his narrative, Smith accentuates his yearnings for approval and assimilation into American society. Moreover, he ultimately expresses his utter and disheartening disappointments that even his material success does not remove the limitations he faces because of his race. No matter how much property or wealth Smith acquired—he was still a black man. In addition to expressing frustrations about the insurmountable disparity between whites and blacks, Smith continues his narrative with several instances of his being swindled out of money or property by other blacks. He concludes his insightful narrative by briefly describing some of the ailments pertaining to his old age. Venture Smith died in September 1805.

The story of Venture Smith is remarkably uplifting on a number of levels—and melancholy as well. Smith was able to buy his own freedom and effectively achieve the modern day proverbial American Dream for himself and his family. One would assume that Smith was overwhelmed with joy and happiness because of his successful entrepreneurship and real estate investor. However, the dream of affluence cannot override the injustices of a given society. Money could not bring Smith the joy he was seeking, and it is clear by the time he grew old, the former slave seemed full of regrets.

Smith's narrative is not only enlightening, but it has great value in teaching some simple life lessons. The one virtue Venture Smith possessed was persistence. It seems that when he set his mind to do something, he figured a way out to make his endeavors come to fruition.

Although, Venture Smith's *Narrative* has three editions—as previously noted, the first two editions are nearly identical. The third edition is not, as it contains information and sections, and the contributions of another author, which are not included in the previous two printings. The first edition of Smith's *Narrative*, which is found within this tome, is valuable because it was printed at the time of the narration. There is good reason to believe that the *Narrative* as published in 1798 closely reflects Smith's own distinctive voice. Smith was illiterate and certainly had someone help him write his narrative (Elisha Niles). Moreover, at the time his narrative was written, Smith was also very old and on the verge of losing his eyesight. Furthermore, what makes the first edition unique is its untainted sterility. In numerous cases, specific details Smith talks about can be substantiated with contemporary evidence, and more importantly, the tone of his narrative and his emphasis are raw, idiosyncratic, and unusual. Therefore, it is highly unlikely to reflect less editorial alterations or the perspective influence of others.

POEMS BY A SLAVE
GEORGE MOSES HORTON

The second subject of this compilation is George Moses Horton. What makes Horton unique in the paradigm of ex-slave literature is that he was the first published slave poet in America. Unlike Smith, Horton was literate and could read and write. Unbeknownst to his master, Horton engaged in writing poetry even while enslaved.[8]

J. MITCHELL

---

8 Horton, George, *Poems By A Slave*, (1837).

Bibliography

Woodson, Carter G., *Free Negro Owners of Slaves in the United States in 1830: Together with Absentee Ownership of Slaves in the United States in 1830 (1924)*.

30 Years of Lynching in the United States: 1889-1918. Authored by National Association for the Advancement of Colored People, New York: National Association for the Advancement of Colored People, National Office, (1919).

Mitchell, Joe, *Forgotten Black-on-Black Lynching's in America . . ., 1835-1935*. (Forthcoming release).

The *Boston Independent,* February 7, 1916.

A Narrative of the Life and Adventures of Venture: A Native of Africa, But Resident Above Sixty Years in the United States of America. Related by Himself (1st Edition).Authored by Venture Smith, Edited by H. M. Selden (1798)

Horton, George, *Poems By A Slave*, by George Moses Horton, Philadelphia (1837).

Horton, George, *The POETICAL WORKS of GEORGE M. HORTON: The Colored Bard of North-Carolina, to which is prefixed The Life of the Author, Written by Himself.*

Bruner, Peter; *A Slave's Adventures Toward Freedom: Not Fiction, But The True Story Of A Struggle.*

PREPARED FOR PUBLICATION
BY:
HISTORIC PUBLISHING
J. MITCHELL
Slavery Books African American History Resources
J. MITCHELL

©2017
ALL RIGHTS RESERVED

A
NARRATIVE
OF THE
LIFE AND ADVENTURES
OF
VENTURE,
A NATIVE OF AFRICA:

But resident above sixty years in the United States of America.

RELATED BY HIMSELF

FIRST EDITION

New London:
**PRINTED BY C. HOLT, AT THE BEE-OFFICE.
1798.**

PREFACE.

THE following account of the life of VENTURE is a relation of simple facts, in which nothing is added in substance to what he related himself. Many other interesting and curious passages of his life might have been inserted; but on account of the bulk to which they must necessarily have swelled this narrative, they were omitted. If any should suspect the truth of what is here related, they are referred to people now living who are acquainted with most of the facts mentioned in the narrative.

The reader is here presented with an account, not of a renowned politician or warrior, but of an untutored African slave, brought into this Christian country at eight years of age, wholly destitute of all education but what he received in common with other domesticated animals, enjoying no advantages that could lead him to suppose himself superior to the beasts, his fellow servants. And if he shall derive no other advantage from perusing this narrative, he may experience those sensations of shame and indignation, that will prove him to be not wholly destitute of every noble and generous feeling.

The subject of the following pages, had he received only a common education, might have been a man of high respectability and usefulness; and had his education been suited to his genius, he might have been an ornament and an honor to human nature. It may perhaps, not be unpleasing to see the efforts of a great mind wholly uncultivated, enfeebled and depressed by slavery, and struggling under every disadvantage.-- The reader may here see a Franklin and a Washington, in a state of nature, or rather in a state of slavery. Destitute as he is of all education, and broken by hardships and infirmities of age, he still exhibits striking traces of native ingenuity and good sense.

This narrative exhibits a pattern of honesty, prudence and industry, to people of his own colour; and perhaps some white people would not find themselves degraded by imitating such an example.

The following account is published in compliance with the earnest desire of the subject of it, and likewise a number of respectable persons who are acquainted with him.

A NARRATIVE OF THE LIFE, &C.

CHAPTER I.

Containing an account of his life, from his birth to the time of his leaving his native country.

I WAS born at Dukandarra, in Guinea, about the year 1729. My father's name was Saungm Furro, Prince of the Tribe of Dukandarra. My father had three wives. Polygamy was not uncommon in that country, especially among the rich, as every man was allowed to keep as many wives as he could maintain. By his first wife he had three children. The eldest of them was myself, named by my father, Broteer. The other two were named Cundazo and Soozaduka. My father had two children by his second wife, and one by his third. I descended from a very large, tall and stout race of beings, much larger than the generality of people in other parts of the globe, being commonly considerable above six feet in height, and every way well proportioned.

The first thing worthy of notice which I remember was, a contention between my father and mother, on account of my father's marrying his third wife without the consent of his first and eldest, which was contrary to the custom generally observed among my countrymen. In consequence of this rupture, my mother left her husband and country, and travelled away with her three children to the eastward. I was then five years old. She took not the least sustenance along with her, to support either herself or children. I was able to travel along by her side; the other two of her offspring she carried one on her back, and the other being a sucking child, in her arms. When we became hungry, my mother used to set us down on the ground, and gather some of the fruits, which grew spontaneously in that climate. These served us for food on the way. At night we all lay down together in the most secure place we could find, and reposed ourselves until morning. Though there were many noxious animals there; yet so kind was our Almighty protector, that none of them were ever permitted to hurt or molest us. Thus we went on our journey until the second day after our departure from Dukandarra, when we came to the entrance of a great desert. During our travel in that we were often affrighted with the doleful howlings and yellings of wolves, lions, and other animals. After five days travel we came to the end of this desert, and immediately entered into a beautiful and extensive interval country. Here my mother was pleased to stop and seek a refuge for me. She left me at the house of a very rich farmer. I was then, as I should judge, not less than one hundred and forty miles from my native place, separated from all my relations and acquaintance. At this place my mother took her farewell of me, and set out for her own country. My new guardian, as I shall call the man with whom I was left, put me into the business of tending sheep, immediately after I was left with him. The flock, which I kept with the assistance of a boy, consisted of about forty. We drove them every morning between two and three miles to pasture, into the wide and delightful plains. When night drew on, we drove them home and secured them in the cote. In this round I continued during my stay there. One incident, which befell me when I was driving my flock from pasture, was so dreadful to me in that age, and is to this time so fresh in my memory, that I cannot help noticing it in this place. Two large dogs sallied out of a certain house and set upon me. One of them took me by the arm, and the other by the thigh, and before their master could come and relieve me, they lacerated my flesh to such a degree, that the scars are very visible to the present day. My master was immediately sent for. He came and carried me home, as I was unable to go myself on account of my wounds. Nothing remarkable happened afterwards until my father sent for me to return home.

Before I dismiss this country, I must just inform my reader what I remember concerning this place. A large river runs through this country in a westerly course. The land for a great way on each side is flat and level, hedged in by a considerable rise of the country at a great distance from it. It scarce ever rains there, yet the land is fertile; great dews fall in the night, which refresh the soil. About the latter end of June or first of July, the river begins to rise, and gradually increases until it has inundated the country for a great distance, to the height of seven or eight feet. This brings on a slime, which enriches the land surprisingly. When the river has subsided, the natives begin to sow and plant, and the vegetation is exceeding rapid. Near this rich river my guardian's land lay. He possessed, I cannot exactly tell how much, yet this I am certain of respecting it, that he owned an immense tract. He possessed likewise a great many cattle and goats. During my stay with him I was kindly used, and with as much tenderness, for what I saw, as his only son, although I was an entire stranger to him, remote from friends and relations. The principal occupations of the inhabitants there, were the cultivation of the soil and the care of their flocks. They were a people pretty similar in every respect to that of mine, except in their persons, which were not so tall and stout. They appeared to be very kind and friendly. I will now return to my departure from that place.

My father sent a man and horse after me. After settling with my guardian for keeping me, he took me away and went for home. It was then about one year since my mother brought me here. Nothing remarkable occurred to us on our journey until we arrived safe home.

I found then that the difference between my parents had been made up previous to their sending for me. On my return, I was received both by my father and mother with great joy and affection, and was once more restored to my paternal dwelling in peace and happiness. I was then about six years old.

Not more than six weeks had passed after my return, before a message was brought by an inhabitant of the place where I lived the preceding year to my father, that that place had been invaded by a numerous army, from a nation not far distant, furnished with musical instruments, and all kinds of arms then in use; that they were instigated by some white nation who equipped and sent them to subdue and possess the country; that his nation had made no preparation for war, having been for a long time in profound peace that they could not defend themselves against such a formidable train of invaders, and must therefore necessarily evacuate their lands to the fierce enemy, and fly to the protection of some chief; and that if he would permit them they should come under his rule and protection when they had to retreat from their own possessions. He was a kind and merciful prince, and therefore consented to these proposals.

He had scarcely returned to his nation with the message, before the whole of his people were obliged to retreat from their country, and come to my father's dominions.

He gave them every privilege and all the protection his government could afford. But they had not been there longer than four days before news came to them that the invaders had laid waste their country, and were coming speedily to destroy them in my father's territories. This affrighted them, and therefore they immediately pushed off to the southward, into the unknown countries there, and were never more heard of.

Two days after their retreat, the report turned out to be but too true. A detachment from the enemy came to my father and informed him, that the whole army was encamped not far out of his dominions, and would invade the territory and deprive his people of their liberties and rights, if he did not comply with the following terms. These were to pay them a large sum of money, three hundred fat cattle, and a great number of goats, sheep, asses, &c.

My father told the messenger he would comply rather than that his subjects should be deprived of their rights and privileges, which he was not then in circumstances to defend from so sudden an invasion. Upon turning out those articles, the enemy pledged their faith and honor that they would not attack him. On these he relied and therefore thought it unnecessary to be on his guard against the enemy. But their pledges of faith and honor proved no better than those of other unprincipled hostile nations; for a few days after a certain relation of the king came and informed him, that the enemy who sent terms of accommodation to him and received tribute to their satisfaction, yet meditated an attack upon his subjects by surprise, and that probably they would commence their attack in less than one day, and concluded with advising him, as he was not prepared for war, to order a speedy retreat of his family and subjects. He complied with this advice.

The same night, which was fixed upon to retreat, my father, and his family, set off about break of day. The king and his two younger wives went in one company, and my mother and her children in another. We left our dwellings in succession, and my father's company went on first. We directed our course for a large shrub plain, some distance off, where we intended to conceal ourselves from the approaching enemy, until we could refresh and rest ourselves a little. But we presently found that our retreat was not secure. For having struck up a little fire for the purpose of cooking victuals, the enemy who happened to be encamped a little distance off, had sent out a scouting party who discovered us by the smoke of the fire, just as we were extinguishing it, and about to eat. As soon as we had finished eating, my father discovered the party, and immediately began to discharge arrows at them. This was what I first saw, and it alarmed both me and the women, who being unable to make any resistance, immediately betook ourselves to the tall thick reeds not far off, and left the old king to fight alone. For some time I beheld him from the reeds defending himself with great courage and firmness, until at last he was obliged to surrender himself into their hands.

They then came to us in the reeds, and the very first salute I had from them was a violent blow on the head with the fore part of a gun, and at the same time a grasp round the neck. I then had a rope put about my neck, as had all the women in the thicket with me, and were immediately led to my father, who was likewise pinioned and haltered for leading. In this condition we were all led to the camp. The women and myself being pretty submissive, had tolerable treatment from the enemy, while my father was closely interrogated respecting his money, which they knew he must have. But as he gave them no account of it, he was instantly cut and pounded on his body with great inhumanity, that he might be induced by the torture he suffered to make the discovery. All this availed not in the least to make him give up his money, but he despised all the tortures, which they inflicted, until the continued exercise and increase of torment, obliged him to sink and expire. He thus died without informing his enemies of the place where his money lay. I saw him while he was thus tortured to death. The shocking scene is to this day fresh in my mind, and I have often been overcome while thinking on it. He was a man of remarkable stature. I should judge as much as six feet and six or seven inches high, two feet across his shoulders, and every way well proportioned. He was a man of remarkable strength and resolution, affable, kind and gentle, ruling with equity and moderation.

The army of the enemy was large, I should suppose consisting of about six thousand men. Their leader was called Baukurre. After destroying the old prince, they decamped and immediately marched towards the sea, lying to the west, taking with them myself and the women prisoners. In the march a scouting party was detached from the main army. To the leader of this party I was made waiter, having to carry his gun, &c.--As we were a scouting we came across a herd of fat cattle, consisting of about thirty in number. These we set upon, and immediately wrested from their keepers, and afterwards converted them into food for the army. The enemy had remarkable success in destroying the country wherever they went. For as far as they had penetrated, they laid the habitations waste and captured the people. The distance they had now brought me was about four hundred miles. All the march I had very hard tasks imposed on me, which I must perform on pain of punishment. I was obliged to carry on my head a large flat stone used for grinding our corn, weighing as I should suppose, as much as 25 pounds; besides victuals, mat and cooking utensils. Though I was pretty large and stout of my age, yet these burthens were very grievous to me, being only about six years and an half old.

We were then come to a place called Malagasco.--When we entered the place we could not see the least appearance of either houses or inhabitants, but upon stricter search found, that instead of houses above ground they had dens in the sides of hillocks, contiguous to ponds and streams of water. In these we perceived they had all hid themselves, as I suppose they usually did upon such occasions. In order to compel them to surrender, the enemy contrived to smoke them out with faggots. These they put to the entrance of the caves and set them on fire. While they were engaged in this business, to their great surprise some of them were desperately wounded with arrows which fell from above on them. This mystery they soon found out. They perceived that the enemy discharged these arrows through holes on the top of the dens directly into the air.--Their weight brought them back, point downwards on their enemies heads, whilst they were smoking the inhabitants out. The points of their arrows were poisoned, but their enemy had an antidote for it, which they instantly applied to the wounded part. The smoke at last obliged the people to give themselves up. They came out of their caves, first spatting the palms of their hands together, and immediately after extended their arms, crossed at their wrists, ready to be bound and pinioned. I should judge that the dens above mentioned were extended about eight feet horizontally into the earth, six feet in height and as many wide. They were arched over head and lined with earth, which was of the clay kind, and made the surface of their walls firm and smooth.

The invaders then pinioned the prisoners of all ages and sexes indiscriminately, took their flocks and all their effects, and moved on their way towards the sea. On the march the prisoners were treated with clemency, on account of their being submissive and humble. Having come to the next tribe, the enemy laid siege and immediately took men, women, children, flocks, and all their valuable effects. They then went on to the next district which was contiguous to the sea, called in Africa, Anamaboo. The enemies provisions were then almost spent, as well as their strength. The inhabitants knowing what conduct they had pursued, and what were their present intentions, improved the favorable opportunity, attacked them, and took enemy, prisoners; flocks and all their effects. I was then taken a second time. All of us were then put into the castle, and kept for market. On a certain time I and other prisoners were put on board a canoe, under our master, and rowed away to a vessel belonging to Rhode-Island, commanded by capt. Collingwood, and the mate Thomas Mumford. While we were going to the vessel, our master told us all to appear to the best possible advantage for sale. I was bought on board by one Robertson Mumford, steward of said vessel, for four gallons of rum, and a piece of calico, and called VENTURE, on account of his having purchased me with his own private venture. Thus I came by my name. All the slaves that were bought for that vessel's cargo, were two hundred and sixty.

CHAPTER II.

Containing an account of his life, from the time of his leaving Africa, to that of his becoming free.

AFTER all the business was ended on the coast of Africa, the ship sailed from thence to Barbadoes. After an ordinary passage, except great mortality by the small pox, which broke out on board, we arrived at the island of Barbadoes: but when we reached it, there were found out of the two hundred and sixty that sailed from Africa, not more than two hundred alive. These were all sold, except myself and three more, to the planters there.

The vessel then sailed for Rhode-Island, and arrived there after a comfortable passage. Here my master sent me to live with one of his sisters, until he could carry me to Fisher's Island, the place of his residence. I had then completed my eighth year. After staying with his sister some time I was taken to my master's place to live.

When we arrived at Narraganset, my master went ashore in order to return a part of the way by land, and gave me the charge of the keys of his trunks on board the vessel, and charged me not to deliver them up to any body, not even to his father without his orders. To his directions I promised faithfully to conform. When I arrived with my master's articles at his house, my master's father asked me for his son's keys, as he wanted to see what his trunks contained. I told him that my master intrusted me with the care of them until he should return, and that I had given him my word to be faithful to the trust, and could not therefore give him or any other person the keys without my master's directions. He insisted that I should deliver to him the keys, threatening to punish me if I did not. But I let him know that he should not have them let him say what he would. He then laid aside trying to get them. But notwithstanding he appeared to give up trying to obtain them from me, yet I mistrusted that he would take some time when I was off my guard, either in the day time or at night to get them, therefore I slung them round my neck, and in the day time concealed them in my bosom, and at night I always lay with them under me, that no person might take them from me without being apprized of it. Thus I kept the keys from every body until my master came home. When he returned he asked where VENTURE was. As I was then within hearing, I came, and said, here sir, at your service. He asked me for his keys, and I immediately took them off my neck and reached them out to him. He took them, stroked my hair, and commended me, saying in presence of his father that his young VENTURE was so faithful that he never would have been able to have taken the keys from him but by violence; that he should not fear to trust him with his whole fortune, for that he had been in his native place so habituated to keeping his word, that he would sacrifice even his life to maintain it.

The first of the time of living at my master's own place, I was pretty much employed in the house at carding wool and other household business. In this situation I continued for some years, after which my master put me to work out of doors. After many proofs of my faithfulness and honesty, my master began to put great confidence in me. My behavior to him had as yet been submissive and obedient. I then began to have hard tasks imposed on me. Some of these were to pound four bushels of ears of corn every night in a barrel for the poultry, or be rigorously punished. At other seasons of the year I had to card wool until a very late hour. These tasks I had to perform when I was about nine years old. Some time after I had another difficulty and oppression, which was greater than any I had ever experienced since I came into this country. This was to serve two masters. James Mumford, my master's son, when his father had gone from home in the morning, and given me a stint to perform that day, would order me to do *this* and *that* business different from what my master directed me.

One day in particular, the authority, which my master's son had set up, had like to have produced melancholy effects. For my master having set me off my business to perform that day and then left me to perform it, his son came up to me in the course of the day, big with authority, and commanded me very arrogantly to quit my present business and go directly about what he should order me. I replied to him that my master had given me so much to perform that day, and that I must therefore faithfully complete it in that time. He then broke out into a great rage, snatched a pitchfork and went to lay me over the head therewith; but I as soon got another and defended myself with it, or otherwise be might have murdered me in his outrage. He immediately called some people who were within hearing at work for him, and ordered them to take his hair rope and come and bind me with it. They all tried to bind me but in vain, tho' there were three assistants in number. My upstart master then desisted, put his pocket handkerchief before his eyes and went home with a design to tell his mother of the struggle with young VENTURE. He told her that their young VENTURE had become so stubborn that he could not controul him, and asked her what he should do with him. In the mean time I recovered my temper, voluntarily caused myself to be bound by the same men who tried in vain before, and carried before my young master, that he might do what he pleased with me. He took me to a gallows made for the purpose of hanging cattle on, and suspended me on it. Afterwards he ordered one of his hands to go to the peach orchard and cut him three dozen of whips to punish me with. These were brought to him, and that was all that was done with them, as I was released and went to work after hanging on the gallows about an hour.

After I had lived with my master thirteen years, being then about twenty two years old, I married Meg, a slave of his who was about my age. My master owned a certain Irishman, named Heddy, who about that time formed a plan of secretly leaving his master. After he had long had this plan in meditation he suggested it to me. At first I cast a deaf ear to it, and rebuked Heddy for harboring in his mind such a rash undertaking. But after he had persuaded and much enchanted me with the prospect of gaining my freedom by such a method, I at length agreed to accompany him. Heddy next inveigled two of his fellow servants to accompany us. The place to which we designed to go was the Mississippi. Our next business was to lay in a sufficient store of provisions for our voyage. We privately collected out of our master's store, six great old cheeses, two firkins of butter, and one whole batch of new bread. When we had gathered all our own clothes and some more, we took them all about midnight, and went to the water side. We stole our master's boat, embarked, and then directed our course for the Mississippi river.

We mutually confederated not to betray or desert one another on pain of death. We first steered our course for Montauk point, the east end of Long-Island. After our arrival there we landed, and Heddy and I made an incursion into the island after fresh water, while our two comrades were left at a little distance from the boat, employed at cooking. When Heddy and I had sought some time for water, he returned to our companions, and I continued on looking for my object. When Heddy had performed his business with our companions who were engaged in cooking, he went directly to the boat, stole all the clothes in it, and then travelled away for East-Hampton, as I was informed. I returned to my fellows not long after. They informed me that our clothes were stolen, but could not determine who was the thief, yet they suspected Heddy as he was missing. After reproving my two comrades for not taking care of our things which were in the boat, I advertised Heddy and sent two men in search of him. They pursued and overtook him at Southampton and returned him to the boat. I then thought it might afford some chance for my freedom, or at least a palliation for my running away, to return Heddy immediately to his master, and inform him that I was induced to go away by Heddy's address. Accordingly I set off with him and the rest of my companions for our master's, and arrived there without any difficulty. I informed my master that Heddy was the ringleader of our revolt, and that he had used us ill. He immediately put Heddy into custody, and myself and companions were well received and went to work as usual.

Not a long time passed after that, before Heddy was sent by my master to New-London gaol. At the close of that year I was sold to a Thomas Stanton, and had to be separated from my wife and one daughter, who was about one month old. He resided at Stonington-point. To this place I brought with me from my late master's, two johannes, three old Spanish dollars, and two thousand of coppers, besides five pounds of my wife's money. This money I got by cleaning gentlemen's shoes and drawing boots, by catching musk-rats and minks, raising potatoes and carrots, &c. and by fishing in the night, and at odd spells.

All this money amounting to near twenty-one pounds York currency, my master's brother, Robert Stanton, hired of me, for which he gave me his note. About one year and a half after that time, my master purchased my wife and her child, for seven hundred pounds old tenor. One time my master sent me two miles after a barrel of molasses, and ordered me to carry it on my shoulders. I made out to carry it all the way to my master's house. When I lived with Captain George Mumford, only to try my strength, I took up on my knees a tierce of salt containing seven bushels, and carried it two or three rods. Of this fact there are several eye witnesses now living.

Towards the close of the time that I resided with this master, I had a falling out with my mistress. This happened one time when my master was gone to Long-Island a gunning. At first the quarrel began between my wife and her mistress. I was then at work in the barn, and hearing a racket in the house, induced me to run there and see what had broken out. When I entered the house, I found my mistress in a violent passion with my wife, for what she informed me was a mere trifle; such a small affair that I forbear to put my mistress to the shame of having it known. I earnestly requested my wife to beg pardon of her mistress for the sake of peace, even if she had given no just occasion for offence. But whilst I was thus saying my mistress turned the blows which she was repeating on my wife to me. She took down her horse-whip, and while she was glutting her fury with it, I reached out my great black hand, raised it up and received the blows of the whip on it which were designed for my head. Then I immediately committed the whip to the devouring fire.

When my master returned from the island, his wife told him of the affair, but for the present he seemed to take no notice of it, and mentioned not a word about it to me. Some days after his return, in the morning as I was putting on a log in the fire-place, not suspecting harm from any one, I received a most violent stroke on the crown of my head with a club two feet long and as large round as a chair-post. This blow very badly wounded my head, and the scar of it remains to this day. The first blow made me have my wits about me you may suppose, for as soon as he went to renew it, I snatched the club out of his hands and dragged him out of the door. He then sent for his brother to come and assist him, but I presently left my master, took the club he wounded me with, carried it to a neighboring Justice of the Peace, and complained of my master. He finally advised me to return to my master, and live contented with him till he abused me again, and then complain. I consented to do accordingly. But before I set out for my master's, up he come and his brother Robert after me. The Justice improved this convenient opportunity to caution my master. He asked him for what he treated his slave thus hastily and unjustly, and told him what would be the consequence if he continued the same treatment towards me. After the Justice had ended his discourse with my master, he and his brother set out with me for home, one before and the other behind me. When they had come to a bye place, they both dismounted their respective horses, and fell to beating me with great violence. I became enraged at this and immediately turned them both under me, laid one of them across the other, and stamped both with my feet what I would.

This occasioned my master's brother to advise him to put me off. A short time after this I was taken by a constable and two men. They carried me to a blacksmith's shop and had me hand-cuffed. When I returned home my mistress enquired much of her waiters, whether VENTURE was hand-cuffed. When she was informed that I was, she appeared to be very contented and was much transported with the news. In the midst of this content and joy, I presented myself before my mistress, shewed her my hand-cuffs, and gave her thanks for my gold rings. For this my master commanded a negro of his to fetch him a large ox chain. This my master locked on my legs with two padlocks. I contitinued to wear the chain peaceably for two or three days, when my master asked me with contemptuous hard names whether I had not better be freed from my chains and go to work. I answered him, No. Well then, said me, I will send you to the West-Indies or banish you, for I am resolved not to keep you. I answered him I crossed the waters to come here, and I am willing to cross them to return.

For a day or two after this not any one said much to me, until one Hempsted Miner, of Stonington, asked me if I would live with him. I answered him that I would. He then requested me to make myself discontented and to appear as unreconciled to my master as I could before that he bargained with him for me; and that in return he would give me a good chance to gain my freedom when I came to live with him. I did as he requested me. Not long after Hempsted Miner purchased me of my master for fifty-six pounds lawful. He took the chain and padlocks from off me immediately after.

It may here be remembered, that I related a few pages back, that I hired out a sum of money to Mr. Robert Stanton, and took his note for it. In the fray between my master Stanton and myself, he broke open my chest containing his brother's note to me, and destroyed it. Immediately after my present master bought me, he determined to sell me at Hartford. As soon as I became apprized of it, I bethought myself that I would secure a certain sum of money which lay by me, safer than to hire it out to a Stanton. Accordingly

I buried it in the earth, a little distance from Thomas Stanton's, in the road over which he passed daily. A short time after my master carried me to Hartford, and first proposed to sell me to one William Hooker of that place. Hooker asked whether I would go to the German Flats with him. I answered, No. He said I should, if not by fair means I should by foul. If you will go by no other measures, I will tie you down in my sleigh. I replied to him, that if he carried me in that manner, no person would purchase me, for it would be thought that he had a murderer for sale. After this he tried no more, and said he would not have me as a gift.

My master next offered me to Daniel Edwards, Esq. of Hartford, for sale. But not purchasing me, my master pawned me to him for ten pounds, and returned to Stonington. After some trial of my honesty, Mr. Edwards placed considerable trust and confidence in me. He put me to serve as his cup-bearer and waiter. When there was company at his house, he would send me into his cellar and other parts of his house to fetch wine and other articles occasionally for them. When I had been with him some time, he asked me why my master wished to part with such an honest negro, and why he did not keep me himself. I replied that I could not give him the reason, unless it was to convert me into cash, and speculate with me as with other commodities.

I hope that he can never justly say it was on account of my ill conduct that he did not keep me himself. Mr. Edwards told me that he should be very willing to keep me himself, and that he would never let me go from him to live, if it was not unreasonable and inconvenient for me to be parted from my wife and children; therefore he would furnish me with a horse to return to Stonington, if I had a mind for it. As Miner did not appear to redeem me I went, and called at my old master Stanton's first to see my wife, who was then owned by him. As my old master appeared much ruffled at my being there, I left my wife before I had spent any considerable time with her, and went to Colonel O. Smith's. Miner had not as yet wholly settled with Stanton for me, and had before my return from Hartford given Col. Smith a bill of sale of me. These men once met to determine which of them should hold me, and upon my expressing a desire to be owned by Col. Smith, and upon my master's settling the remainder of the money which was due to Stanton for me, it was agreed that I should live with Col. Smith.

This was the third time of my being sold, and I was then thirty-one years old. As I never had an opportunity of redeeming myself whilst I was owned by Miner, though he promised to give me a chance, I was then very ambitious of obtaining it. I asked my master one time if he would consent to have me purchase my freedom. He replied that he would. I was then very happy, knowing that I was at that time able to pay part of the purchase money, by means of the money which I some time since buried. This I took out of the earth and tendered to my master, having previously engaged a free negro man to take his security for it, as I was the property of my master, and therefore could not safely take his obligation myself. What was wanting in redeeming myself, my master agreed to wait on me for, until I could procure it for him. I still continued to work for Col. Smith. There was continually some interest accruing on my master's note to my friend the free negro man above named, which I received, and with some besides which I got by fishing, I laid out in land adjoining my old master Stanton's. By cultivating this land with the greatest diligence and economy, at times when my master did not require my labor, in two years I laid up ten pounds. This my friend tendered my master for myself, and received his note for it.

Being encouraged by the success which I had met in redeeming myself, I again solicited my master for a further chance of completing it. The chance for which I solicited him was that of going out to work the ensuing winter. He agreed to this on condition that I would give him one quarter of my earnings. On these terms I worked the following winter, and earned four pounds sixteen shillings, one quarter of which went to my master for the privilege, and the rest was paid him on my own account. This added to the other payments made up forty four pounds, eight shillings, which I had paid on my own account. I was then about thirty five years old.

The next summer I again desired he would give me a chance of going out to work. But he refused and answered that he must have my labor this summer, as he did not have it the past winter. I replied that I considered it as hard that I could not have a chance to work out when the season became advantageous, and that I must only be permitted to hire myself out in the poorest season of the year. He asked me after this what I would give him for the privilege per month. I replied that I would leave it wholly with his own generosity to determine what I should return him a month. Well then, said he, if so two pounds a month. I answered him that if that was the least he would take I would be contented.

Accordingly I hired myself out at Fisher's Island, and earned twenty pounds; thirteen pounds six shillings of which my master drew for the privilege, and the remainder I paid him for my freedom. This made fifty-one pounds two shillings which I paid him. In October following I went and wrought six months at Long Island. In that six month's time I cut and corded four hundred cords of wood, besides threshing out seventy-five bushels of grain, and received of my wages down only twenty pounds, which left remaining a larger sum. Whilst I was out that time, I took up on my wages only one pair of shoes. At night I lay on the hearth, with one coverlet over and another under me. I returned to my master and gave him what I received of my six months labor. This left only thirteen pounds eighteen shillings to make up the full sum for my redemption. My master liberated me, saying that I might pay what was behind if I could ever make it convenient, otherwise it would be well. The amount of the money which I had paid my master towards redeeming my time, was seventy-one pounds two shillings. The reason of my master for asking such an unreasonable price, was he said, to secure himself in case I should ever come to want. Being thirty-six years old, I left Col. Smith once for all. I had already been sold three different times, made considerable money with seemingly nothing to derive it from, been cheated out of a large sum of money, lost much by misfortunes, and paid an enormous sum for my freedom.

CHAPTER III.

Containing an account of his life, from the time of his purchasing his freedom to the present day.

MY wife and children were yet in bondage to Mr. Thomas Stanton. About this time I lost a chest, containing besides clothing, about thirty-eight pounds in paper money. It was burnt by accident. A short time after I sold all my possessions at Stonington, consisting of a pretty piece of land and one dwelling house thereon, and went to reside at Long-Island. For the first four years of my residence there, I spent my time in working for various people on that and at the neighboring islands. In the space of six months I cut and corded upwards of four hundred cords of wood. Many other singular and wonderful labors I performed in cutting wood there, which would not be inferior to those just recited, but for brevity sake I must omit them. In the aforementioned four years what wood I cut at Long-Island amounted to several thousand cords, and the money which I earned thereby amounted to two hundred and seven pounds ten shillings. This money I laid up carefully by me. Perhaps some may enquire what maintained me all the time I was laying up money.

I would inform them that I bought nothing which I did not absolutely want. All fine clothes I despised in comparison with my interest, and never kept but just what clothes were comfortable for common days, and perhaps I would have a garment or two which I did not have on at all times, but as for superfluous finery I never thought it to be compared with a decent homespun dress, a good supply of money and prudence. Expensive gatherings of my mates I commonly shunned, and all kinds of luxuries I was perfectly a stranger to; and during the time I was employed in cutting the aforementioned quantity of wood, I never was at the expence of six-pence worth of spirits. Being after this labour forty years of age, I worked at various places, and in particular on Ram-Island, where I purchased Solomon and Cuff, two sons of mine, for two hundred dollars each.

It will here be remembered how much money I earned by cutting wood in four years. Besides this I had considerable money, amounting in all to near three hundred pounds. When I had purchased my two sons, I had then left more than one hundred pounds. After this I purchased a negro man, for no other reason than to oblige him, and gave for him sixty pounds. But in a short time after he run away from me, and I thereby lost all that I gave for him, except twenty pounds which he paid me previous to his absconding. The rest of my money I laid out in land, in addition to a farm which I owned before, and a dwelling house thereon. Forty four years had then completed their revolution since my entrance into this existence of servitude and misfortune. Solomon my eldest son, being then in his seventeenth year, and all my hope and dependence for help, I hired him out to one Charles Church, of Rhode-Island, for one year, on consideration of his giving him twelve pounds and an opportunity of acquiring some learning. In the course of the year, Church fitted out a vessel for a whaling voyage, and being in want of hands to man her, he induced my son to go, with the promise of giving him on his return, a pair of silver buckles, besides his wages. As soon as I heard of his going to sea, I immediately set out to go and prevent it if possible.--But on my arrival at Church's, to my great grief, I could only see the vessel my son was in almost out of sight going to sea. My son died of the scurvy in this voyage, and Church has never yet paid me the least of his wages. In my son, besides the loss of his life, I lost equal to seventy-five pounds.

My other son being but a youth, still lived with me. About this time I chartered a sloop of about thirty tons burthen, and hired men to assist me in navigating her. I employed her mostly in the wood trade to Rhode-Island, and made clear of all expences above one hundred dollars with her in better than one year. I had then become something forehanded, and being in my forty-fourth year, I purchased my wife Meg, and thereby prevented having another child to buy, as she was then pregnant. I gave forty pounds for her.

During my residence at Long-Island, I raised one year with another, ten cart loads of water-melons, and lost a great many every year besides by the thievishness of the sailors. What I made by the water-melons I sold there, amounted to nearly five hundred dollars. Various other methods I pursued in order to enable me to redeem my family. In the night time I fished with set-nets and pots for eels and lobsters, and shortly after went a whaling voyage in the service of Col. Smith.--After being out seven months, the vessel returned, laden with four hundred barrels of oil. About this time, I become possessed of another dwelling-house, and my temporal affairs were in a pretty prosperous condition. This and my industry was what alone saved me from being expelled that part of the island in which I resided, as an act was passed by the select-men of the place, that all negroes residing there should be expelled.

Next after my wife, I purchased a negro man for four hundred dollars. But he having an inclination to return to his old master, I therefore let him go. Shortly after I purchased another negro man for twenty-five pounds, whom I parted with shortly after.

Being about forty-six years old, I bought my oldest child Hannah, of Ray Mumford, for forty-four pounds, and she still resided with him. I had already redeemed from slavery, myself, my wife and three children, besides three negro men.

About the forty-seventh year of my life, I disposed of all my property at Long-Island, and came from thence into East-Haddam: I hired myself out at first to Timothy Chapman, for five weeks, the earnings of which time I put up carefully by me. After this I wrought for Abel Bingham about six weeks. I then put my money together and purchased of said Bingham ten acres of land, lying at Haddam neck, where I now reside.--On this land I labored with great diligence for two years, and shortly after purchased six acres more of land contiguous to my other. One year from that time I purchased seventy acres more of the same man, and paid for it mostly with the produce of my other land. Soon after I bought this last lot of land, I set up a comfortable dwelling house on my farm, and built it from the produce thereof. Shortly after I had much trouble and expence with my daughter Hannah, whose name has before been mentioned in this account. She was married soon after I redeemed her, to one Isaac, a free negro, and shortly after her marriage fell sick of a mortal disease; her husband a dissolute and abandoned wretch, paid but little attention to her in her illness. I therefore thought it best to bring her to my house and nurse her there. I procured her all the aid mortals could afford, but notwithstanding this she fell a prey to her disease, after a lingering and painful endurance of it.

The physician's bills for attending her during her illness amounted to forty pounds. Having reached my fifty-fourth year, a hired two negro men, one named William Jacklin, and the other Mingo. Mingo lived with me one year, and having received his wages, run in debt to me eight dollars, for which he gave me his note. Presently after he tried to run away from me without troubling himself to pay up his note. I procured a warrant, took him, and requested him to go to Justice Throop's of his own accord, but he refusing, I took him on my shoulders, and carried him there; distant

about two miles. The justice asking me if I had my prisoner's note with me, and replying that I had not, he told me that I must return with him and get it. Accordingly I carried Mingo back on my shoulders, but before we arrived at my dwelling, he complained of being hurt, and asked me if this was not a hard way of treating our fellow creatures. I answered him that it would be hard thus to treat our honest fellow creatures. He then told me that if I would let him off my shoulders, he had a pair of silver shoe-buckles, one shirt and a pocket handkerchief, which he would turn out to me. I agreed, and let him return home with me on foot; but the very following night, he slipped from me, stole my horse and has never paid me even his note. The other negro man, Jacklin, being a comb-maker by trade, he requested me to set him up, and promised to reward me well with his labor. Accordingly I bought him a set of tools for making combs, and procured him stock. He worked at my house about one year, and then run away from me with all his combs, and owed me for all his board.

Since my residence at Haddam neck, I have owned of boats, canoes and sail vessels, not less than twenty. These I mostly employed in the fishing and trafficking business, and in these occupations I have been cheated out of considerable money by people whom I traded with taking advantage of my ignorance of numbers.

About twelve years ago, I hired a whale-boat and four black men, and proceeded to Long-Island after a load of round clams. Having arrived there, I first purchased of James Webb, son of Orange Webb, six hundred and sixty clams, and afterwards, with the help of my men, finished loading my boat. The same evening, however, this Webb stole my boat, and went in her to Connecticut river, and sold her cargo for his own benefit. I thereupon pursued him, and at length, after an additional expence of nine crowns, recovered the boat; but for the proceeds of her cargo I never could obtain any compensation.

Four years after, I met with another loss, far superior to this in value, and I think by no less wicked means. Being going to New-London with a grand-child, I took passage in an Indian's boat, and went there with him. On our return, the Indian took on board two hogsheads of molasses, one of which belonged to Capt. Elisha Hart, of Saybrook, to be delivered on his wharf. When we arrived there, and while I was gone, at the request of the Indian, to inform Captain Hart of his arrival, and receive the freight for him, one hogshead of the molasses had been lost overboard by the people in attempting to land it on the wharf. Although I was absent at the time, and had no concern whatever in the business, as was known to a number of respectable witnesses, I was nevertheless prosecuted by this conscientious gentleman, (the Indian not being able to pay for it) and obliged to pay upwards of ten pounds lawful money, with all the costs of court. I applied to several gentlemen for counsel in this affair, and they advised me, as my adversary was rich, and threatened to carry the matter from court to court till it would cost me more than the first damages would be to pay the sum and submit to the injury; which I according did, and he has often since insultingly taunted me with my unmerited misfortune. Such a proceeding as this, committed on a defenceless stranger, almost worn out in the hard service of the world, without any foundation in reason or justice, whatever it may be called in a christian land, would in my native country have been branded as a crime equal to highway robbery. But Captain Hart was a *white gentleman,* and I a *poor African,* therefore it was *all right, and good enough for the black dog.*

I am now sixty nine years old. Though once strait and tall, measuring without shoes six feet one inch and an half, and every way well proportioned, I am now bowed down with age and hardship. My strength which was once equal if not superior to any man whom I have ever seen, is now enfeebled so that life is a burden, and it is with fatigue that I can walk a couple of miles, stooping over my staff. Other griefs are still behind, on account of which some aged people, at least, will pity me. My eye-sight has gradually failed, till I am almost blind, and whenever I go abroad one of my grand-children must direct my way; besides for many years I have been much pained and troubled with an ulcer on one of my legs.

But amidst all my griefs and pains, I have many consolations; Meg, the wife of my youth, whom I married for love, and bought with my money, is still alive. My freedom is a privilege which nothing else can equal. Notwithstanding all the losses I have suffered by fire, by the injustice of knaves, by the cruelty and oppression of false hearted friends, and the perfidy of my own countrymen whom I have assisted and redeemed from bondage, I am now possessed of more than one hundred acres of land, and three habitable dwelling houses. It gives me joy to think that I *have* and that I *deserve* so good a character, especially for *truth* and *integrity*. While I am now looking to the grave as my home, my joy for this world would be full--IF my children, Cuff for whom I paid two hundred dollars when a boy, and Solomon who was born soon after I purchased his mother--If Cuff and Solomon--O! that they had walked in the way of their father. But a father's lips are closed in silence and in grief!--Vanity of vanities, all is vanity!

FINIS

CERTIFICATE.

STONINGTON, November 3, 1793.

THESE certify, that VENTURE, a free negro man, aged about 69 years, and was, as we have ever understood, a native of Africa, and formerly a slave to Mr. James Mumford, of Fisher's-Island, in the state of New-York; who sold him to Mr. Thomas Stanton, 2d, of Stonington, in the state of Connecticut, and said Stanton sold said VENTURE to Col. Oliver Smith, of the aforesaid place. That said VENTURE hath sustained the character of a faithful servant, and that of a temperate, honest and industrious man, and being ever intent on obtaining his freedom, he was indulged by his masters after the ordinary labour on the days of his servitude, to improve the nights in fishing and other employments to his own emolument, in which time he procured so much money as to purchase his freedom from his late master Col. Smith; after which he took upon himself the name of VENTURE SMITH, and has since his freedom purchased a negro woman, called Meg, to whom he was previously married, and also his children who were slaves, and said VENTURE has since removed himself and family to the town of East-Haddam, in this state, where he hath purchased lands on which he hath built a house, and there taken up his abode.

NATHANIEL MINOR, Esq.
ELIJAH PALMER, Esq.
Capt. AMOS PALMER,
ACORS SHEFFIELD,
EDWARD SMITH

57

POEMS BY A SLAVE

By

George Moses Horton

Second Edition

Philadelphia
1837

PREPARED FOR PUBLICATION
BY
HISTORIC PUBLISHING

HISTORIC PUBLISHING
SAN ANTONIO, TEXAS
©2017

61

POEMS BY A SLAVE.

EXPLANATION.

GEORGE, who is the author of the following poetical effusions, is a Slave, the property of Mr. James Horton, of Chatham County, North Carolina. He has been in the habit, some years past, of producing poetical pieces, sometimes on suggested subjects, to such persons as would write them while he dictated. Several compositions of his have already appeared in the Raleigh Register. Some have made their way into the Boston newspapers, and have evoked expressions of approbation and surprise. Many persons have now become much interested in the promotion of his prospects, some of whom are elevated in office and literary attainments. They are solicitous that efforts at length be made to obtain by subscription, a sum sufficient for his emancipation, upon the condition of his going in the vessel which shall first afterwards sail for Liberia. It is his earnest and only wish to become a member of that Colony, to enjoy its privileges, and apply his industry and mental abilities to the promotion of its prospects and his own. It is upon these terms alone, that the efforts of those who befriend his views are intended to have a final effect.

To put to trial the plan here urged in his behalf, the paper now exhibited is published. Several of his productions are contained in the succeeding pages. Many more might have been added, which would have swelled into a larger size. They would doubtless be interesting to many, but it is hoped that the specimens here inserted will be sufficient to accomplish the object of the publication. Expense will thus be avoided, and the money better employed in enlarging the sum applicable for his emancipation.--It is proposed, that in every town or vicinity where contributions are made, they may be put into the hands of some person, who will humanely consent to receive them, and give notice to Mr. *Weston R. Gales*, in Raleigh, of the amount collected. As soon as it is ascertained that the collections will accomplish the object, it is expected that they will be transmitted without delay to Mr. *Weston R. Gales*. But should they ultimately prove insufficient, they will be returned to subscribers.

None will imagine it possible that pieces produced as these have been, should be free from blemish in composition or taste. The author is now 32 years of age, and has always laboured in the field on his master's farm, promiscuously with the few others which Mr. Horton owns, in circumstances of the greatest possible simplicity. His master says he knew nothing of his poetry, but as he heard of it from others. GEORGE knows how to read, and is now learning to write. All his pieces are written down by others; and his reading, which is done at night, and at the usual intervals allowed to slaves, has been much employed on poetry, such as he could procure, this being the species of composition most interesting to him. It is thought best to print his productions without correction, that the mind of the reader may be in no uncertainty as to the originality and genuineness of every part. We shall conclude this account of GEORGE, with an assurance that he has been ever a faithful, honest and industrious slave. That his heart has felt deeply and sensitively in this lowest possible condition of human nature, will easily be believed, and is impressively confirmed by one of his stanzas,

> Come, melting Pity, from afar,
> And break this vast enormous bar
> Between a wretch and thee;
> Purchase a few short days of time,
> And bid a vassal soar sublime,
> On wings of Liberty.

Raleigh, July 2, 1829.

PREFACE TO THE SECOND EDITION.

Of these poems, the present publisher has never seen or heard of but one copy, which was recently obtained by JOSHUA COFFIN, of this city, from a gentleman who met with it in Cincinnati a few years ago. The pamphlet is republished, without any alterations,--even verbal; except the insertion of the headline, "Poems by a slave," over the pages, and the omission of the title page, which ran as follows:

"The Hope of Liberty, containing a number of poetical pieces. By George M. Horton. Raleigh, printed by Gales & Son, 1829."

Observe 1st, That Gales, the printer of the pamphlet, is now one of the firm of Gales & Seaton, at Washington,--*no abolitionist.* 2nd, The publisher admits slavery to be "the lowest possible condition of human nature;" and that the slaves are not all happy, for George "felt deeply and sensitively." 3d, The man who could write such poems was kept for 32 years in "the lowest possible condition of human nature," and was to remain there if he would not consent to go to Liberia.

Whether the poems sold for sufficient to buy this man, so dangerous to "Southern institutions," and export him, I have not been able to ascertain. Perhaps George is still a slave!

L. C. G.

Philadelphia, September, 1837.

Immediately after the present edition was issued, the following letter was put into my hands.

PUBLISHER.

Washington, September 12th, 1837.

DEAR SIR:--I have inquired of Mr. Gales, agreeably to your request to ascertain the present condition of *George M. Horton.* He informs me that he is still the slave of James Horton of Chatham County, and is employed as a servant at Chapel Hill, the seat of the University of North Carolina. It is understood by Mr. G. that he did not derive much pecuniary profit from the publication of his poems; and that, since the death of his patron, the late Dr. Caldwell, President of the University he has attended to other occupations.

I am,
Yours truly,
* * * *

Mr. JOSHUA COFFIN.

Poems By A Slave

PRAISE OF CREATION.

Creation fires my tongue!
Nature thy anthems raise;
And spread the universal song
Of thy Creator's praise!

Heaven's chief delight was Man
Before Creation's birth--
Ordained with joy to lead the van,
And reign the lord of earth.

When Sin was quite unknown,
And all the woes it brought,
He hailed the morn without a groan
Or one corroding thought.

When each revolving wheel
Assumed its sphere sublime,
Submissive Earth then heard the peal,
And struck the march of time.

The march in Heaven begun,
And splendor filled the skies,
When Wisdom bade the morning Sun
With joy from chaos rise.

The angels heard the tune
Throughout creation ring;
They seized their golden harps as soon
And touched on every string.

When time and space were young,
And music rolled along--
The morning stars together sung,
And Heaven was drown'd in song.

Ye towering eagles soar,
And fan Creation's blaze,
And ye terrific lions roar,
To your Creator's praise.

Responsive thunders roll,
Loud acclamations sound,
And show your Maker's vast control
O'er all the worlds around.

Stupendous mountains smoke,
And lift your summits high,
To him who all your terrors woke,
Dark'ning the sapphire sky.

Now let my muse descend,
To view the march below--
Ye subterraneous worlds attend
And bid your chorus flow.

Ye vast volcanoes yell
Whence fiery cliffs are hurled;
And all ye liquid oceans swell
Beneath the solid world.

Ye cataracts combine,
Nor let the pæan cease--
The universal concert join,
Thou dismal precipice.

But halt my feeble tongue,
My weary muse delays:
But, oh my soul, still float along
Upon the flood of praise!

ON THE SILENCE OF A YOUNG LADY,

On account of the imaginary flight of her suitor.

Oh, heartless dove! mount in the skies,
Spread thy soft wing upon the gale,
Or on thy sacred pinions rise,
Nor brood with silence in the vale.

Breathe on the air thy plaintive note,
Which oft has filled the lonesome grove,
And let thy melting ditty float--
The dirge of long lamented love.

Coo softly to the silent ear,
And make the floods of grief to roll;
And cause by love the sleeping tear,
To wake with sorrow from the soul.

Is it the loss of pleasures past
Which makes thee droop thy sounding wing?
Does winter's rough, inclement blast
Forbid thy tragic voice to sing?

Is it because the fragrant breeze
Along the sky forbears to flow--
Nor whispers low amidst the trees,
Whilst all the vallies frown below?

Why should a frown thy soul alarm,
And tear thy pleasures from thy breast?
Or veil the smiles of every charm,
And rob thee of thy peaceful rest.

Perhaps thy sleeping love may wake,
And hear thy penitential tone;
And suffer not thy heart to break,
Nor let a princess grieve alone.

Perhaps his pity may return,
With equal feeling from the heart,
And breast with breast together burn,
Never--no, never more to part.

Never, till death's resistless blow,
Whose call the dearest must obey--
In twain together then may go,
And thus together dwell for aye.

Say to the suitor, Come away,
Nor break the knot which love has tied--
Nor to the world thy trust betray,
And fly for ever from thy bride.

THE LOVER'S FAREWELL.

And wilt thou, love, my soul display,
And all my secret thoughts betray?
I strove, but could not hold thee fast,
My heart flies off with thee at last.

The favorite daughter of the dawn,
On love's mild breeze will soon be gone;
I strove, but could not cease to love,
Nor from my heart the weight remove.

And wilt thou, love, my soul beguile,
And gull thy fav'rite with a smile?
Nay, soft affection answers, nay,
And beauty wings my heart away.

I steal on tiptoe from these bowers,
All spangled with a thousand flowers;
I sigh, yet leave them all behind,
To gain the object of my mind.

And wilt thou, love, command my soul,
And waft me with a light control?--
Adieu to all the blooms of May,
Farewell--I fly with love away!

I leave my parents here behind,
And all my friends--to love resigned--

'Tis grief to go, but death to stay:
Farewell--I'm gone with love away!

ON LIBERTY AND SLAVERY.

Alas! and am I born for this,
To wear this slavish chain?
Deprived of all created bliss,
Through hardship, toil and pain!

How long have I in bondage lain,
And languished to be free!
Alas! and must I still complain--
Deprived of liberty.

Oh, Heaven! and is there no relief
This side the silent grave--
To soothe the pain--to quell the grief
And anguish of a slave?

Come Liberty, thou cheerful sound,
Roll through my ravished ears!
Come, let my grief in joys be drowned,
And drive away my fears.

Say unto foul oppression, Cease:
Ye tyrants rage no more,
And let the joyful trump of peace,
Now bid the vassal soar.

Soar on the pinions of that dove
Which long has cooed for thee,

And breathed her notes from Afric's grove,
The sound of Liberty.

Oh, Liberty! thou golden prize,
So often sought by blood--
We crave thy sacred sun to rise,
The gift of nature's God!

Bid Slavery hide her haggard face,
And barbarism fly:
I scorn to see the sad disgrace
In which enslaved I lie.

Dear Liberty! upon thy breast,
I languish to respire;
And like the Swan unto her nest,
I'd to thy smiles retire.

Oh, blest asylum--heavenly balm!
Unto thy boughs I flee--
And in thy shades the storm shall calm,
With songs of Liberty!

TO ELIZA.

Eliza, tell thy lover why
 Or what induced thee to deceive me?

Fare thee well--away I fly--
I shun the lass who thus will grieve me.

Eliza, still thou art my song,
Although by force I may forsake thee;

 Fare thee well, for I was wrong
To woo thee while another take thee.

Eliza, pause and think awhile—Sweet lass! I shall forget
thee never:

Fare thee well! although I smile,
I grieve to give thee up for ever.

Eliza, I shall think of thee--
My heart shall ever twine about thee;
Fare thee well--but think of me,
 Compell'd to live and die without thee.
"Fare thee well!--and if for ever,
Still for ever fare thee well!"

LOVE.

Whilst tracing thy visage, I sink in emotion,
For no other damsel so wond'rous I see;
Thy looks are so pleasing, thy charms so amazing,
I think of no other, my true-love, but thee.

With heart-burning rapture I gaze on thy beauty,
And fly like a bird to the boughs of a tree;
Thy looks are so pleasing, thy charms so amazing,
I fancy no other, my true-love, but thee.

Thus oft in the valley I think, and I wonder
Why cannot a maid with her lover agree?
Thy looks are so pleasing, thy charms so amazing,
I pine for no other, my true-love, but thee.

I'd fly from thy frowns with a heart full of sorrow--
Return, pretty damsel, and smile thou on me;
By every endeavour, I'll try thee for ever,
And languish until I am fancied by thee.

ON THE DEATH OF AN INFANT.

Blest Babe! it at length has withdrawn,
The Seraphs have rocked it to sleep;
Away with an angelic smile it has gone,
And left a sad parent to weep!

It soars from the ocean of pain,
On breezes of precious perfume;
O be not discouraged when death is but gain--
The triumph of life from the tomb.

With pleasure I thought it my own,
And smil'd on its infantile charms;
But some mystic bird, like an eagle, came down,
And snatch'd it away from my arms.

Blest Babe, it ascends into Heaven,
It mounts with delight at the call;
And flies to the bosom from whence it was given,
The Parent and Patron of all.

THE SLAVE'S COMPLAINT.

Am I sadly cast aside,
On misfortune's rugged tide?
Will the world my pains deride
For ever?

Must I dwell in Slavery's night,
And all pleasure take its flight,
Far beyond my feeble sight,
For ever?

Worst of all, must Hope grow dim,
And withhold her cheering beam?
Rather let me sleep and dream
For ever!

Something still my heart surveys,
Groping through this dreary maze;
Is it Hope?--then burn and blaze
For ever!

Leave me not a wretch confined,
Altogether lame and blind--
Unto gross despair consigned,
For ever!

Heaven! in whom can I confide?
Canst thou not for all provide?

Condescend to be my guide
For ever:

And when this transient life shall end,
Oh, may some kind, eternal friend
Bid me from servitude ascend,
For ever!

ON THE TRUTH OF THE SAVIOUR.

E'en John the Baptist did not know
Who Christ the Lord could be,
And bade his own disciples go,
The strange event to see.

They said, Art thou the one of whom
'Twas written long before?
Is there another still to come,
Who will all things restore?

This is enough, without a name--
Go, tell him what is done;
Behold the feeble, weak and lame,
With strength rise up and run.

This is enough--the blind now see,
The dumb Hosannas sing;
Devils far from his presence flee,
As shades from morning's wing.

See the distress'd, all bathed in tears,
Prostrate before him fall;
Immanuel speaks, and Lazarus hears--
The dead obeys his call.

This is enough--the fig-tree dies,
And withers at his frown;

Nature her God must recognise,
And drop her flowery crown.

At his command the fish increase,
And loaves of barley swell--
Ye hungry eat, and hold your peace,
And find a remnant still.

At his command the water blushed,
And all was turned to wine,
And in redundance flowed afresh,
And owned its God divine.

Behold the storms at his rebuke,
All calm upon the sea--
How can we for another look,
When none can work as he?

This is enough--it must be God,
From whom the plagues are driven;
At whose command the mountains nod
And all the Host of Heaven!

ON SPRING.

Hail, thou auspicious vernal dawn!
Ye birds, proclaim the winter's gone,
Ye warbling minstrels sing;
Pour forth your tribute as ye rise,
And thus salute the fragrant skies
The pleasing smiles of Spring.

Coo sweetly, oh thou harmless Dove,
And bid thy mate no longer rove,
In cold,hybernal vales;
Let music rise from every tongue,
Whilst winter flies before the song,
Which floats on gentle gales.

Ye frozen streams dissolve and flow
Along the valley, sweet and slow;
Divested fields be gay;
Ye drooping forests bloom on high,
And raise your branches to the sky,
And thus your charms display.

Thou world of heat--thou vital source,
The torpid insects feel thy force,
Which all with life supplies;
Gardens and orchards richly bloom,
And send a gale of sweet perfume,
To invite them as they rise.

Near where the crystal waters glide,

The male of birds escorts his bride,
And twitters on the spray;
He mounts upon his active wing,
To hail the bounty of the Spring,
The lavish pomp of May.

Inspiring month of youthful Love,
How oft we in the peaceful grove,
Survey the flowery plume;
Or sit beneath the sylvan shade,
Where branches wave above the head,
And smile on every bloom.

Exalted month, when thou art gone,
May Virtue then begin the dawn
Of an eternal Spring?
May raptures kindle on my tongue,
And start a new, eternal song,
Which ne'er shall cease to ring!

ON SUMMER.

Esteville fire begins to burn;
The auburn fields of harvest rise;
The torrid flames again return,
And thunders roll along the skies.

Perspiring Cancer lifts his head,
And roars terrific from on high;
Whose voice the timid creatures dread,
From which they strive with awe to fly.

The night-hawk ventures from his cell,
And starts his note in evening air;
He feels the heat his bosom swell,
Which drives away the gloom of fear.

Thou noisy insect, start thy drum;
Rise lamp-like bugs to light the train;
And bid sweet Philomela come,
And sound in front the nightly strain.

The bee begins her ceaseless hum,
And doth with sweet exertions rise;
And with delight she stores her comb,
And well her rising stock supplies.

Let sportive children well beware,
While sprightly frisking o'er the green;

And carefully avoid the snare,
Which lurks beneath the smiling scene.

The mistress bird assumes her nest,
And broods in silence on the tree,
Her note to cease, her wings at rest,
She patient waits her young to see.

The farmer hastens from the heat;
The weary plough-horse droops his head;
The cattle all at noon retreat,
And ruminate beneath the shade.

The burdened ox with dauntless rage,
Flies heedless to the liquid flood,
From which he quaffs, devoid of guage,
Regardless of his driver's rod.

Pomaceous orchards now expand
Their laden branches o'er the lea
And with their bounty fill the land,
While plenty smiles on every tree.

On fertile borders, near the stream,
Now gaze with pleasure and delight;
See loaded vines with melons teem--
'Tis paradise to human sight.

With rapture view the smiling fields,
Adorn the mountain and the plain,

Each, on the eve of Autumn, yields
A large supply of golden grain.

ON WINTER.

When smiling Summer's charms are past,
The voice of music dies;
Then Winter pours his chilling blast
From rough inclement skies.

The pensive dove shuts up her throat,
The larks forbear to soar,
Or raise one sweet, delightful note,
Which charm'd the ear before.

The screech-owl peals her shivering tone
Upon the brink of night;
As some sequestered child unknown,
Which feared to come in sight.

The cattle all desert the field,
And eager seek the glades
Of naked trees, which once did yield
Their sweet and pleasant shades.

The humming insects all are still,
The beetles rise no more,
The constant tinkling of the bell,
Along the health is o'er.

Stern Boreas hurls each piercing gale
With snow-clad wings along,

Discharging volleys mixed with hail
Which chill the breeze of song.

Lo, all the Southern windows close,
Whence spicy breezes roll;
The herbage sinks in sad repose,
And Winter sweeps the whole.

Thus after youth old age comes on,
And brings the frost of time,
And e'er our vigour has withdrawn,
We shed the rose of prime.

Alas! how quick it is the case,
The scion youth is grown--
How soon it runs its morning race,
And beauty's sun goes down.

The Autumn of declining years
Must blanch the father's head,
Encumbered with a load of cares,
When youthful charms have fled.

HEAVENLY LOVE.

Eternal spring of boundless grace,
It lifts the soul above,
Where God the Son unveils his face,
And shows that Heaven is love.

Love that revolves through endless years--
Love that can never pall;
Love which excludes the gloom of fears,
Love to whom God is all!

Love which can ransom every slave,
And set the pris'ner free;
Gild the dark horrors of the grave,
And still the raging sea.

Let but the partial smile of Heaven
Upon the bosom play,
The mystic sound of sins forgiven,
Can waft the soul away.

The pilgrim's spirits show this love,
They often soar on high;
Languish from this dim earth to move.
And leave the flesh to die.

Sing, oh my soul, rise up and run,
And leave this clay behind;

Wing thy swift flight beyond the sun,
Nor dwell in tents confined.

ON THE DEATH OF REBECCA.

Thou delicate blossom! thy short race is ended,
Thou sample of virtue and prize of the brave!
No more are thy beauties by mortals attended,
They now are but food for the worms and the grave.

Thou art gone to the tomb, whence there's no returning.
And left us behind in a vale of suspense;
In vain to the dust do we follow thee mourning,
The same doleful trump will soon call us all hence.

I view thee now launched on eternity's ocean,
Thy soul how it smiles as it floats on the wave;
It smiles as if filled with the softest emotion,
But looks not behind on the frowns of the grave.

The messenger came from afar to relieve thee--
In this lonesome valley no more shalt thou roam;
Bright seraphs now stand on the banks to receive thee,
And cry, "Happy stranger, thou art welcome at home."

Thou art gone to a feast, while thy friends are bewailing,
Oh, death is a song to the poor ransom'd slave;
Away with bright visions the spirit goes sailing,
And leaves the frail body to rest in the grave.

Rebecca is free from the pains of oppression,
No friends could prevail with her longer to stay;

She smiles on the fields of eternal fruition,
Whilst death like a bridegroom attends her away.

She is gone in the whirlwind--ye seraphs attend her,
Through Jordan's cold torrent her mantle may lave,
She soars in the chariot, and earth falls beneath her,
Resign'd in a shroud to a peaceable grave.

ON DEATH.

Deceitful worm, that undermines the clay,
Which slyly steals the thoughtless soul away,
Pervading neighborhoods with sad surprise,
Like sudden storms of wind and thunder rise.

The sounding death-watch lurks within the wall,
Away some unsuspecting soul to call;
The pendant willow droops her waving head,
And sighing zephyrs whisper of the dead.

Methinks I hear the doleful midnight knell--
Some parting spirit bids the world farewell;
The taper burns as conscious of distress,
And seems to show the living number less.

Must a lov'd daughter from her father part,
And grieve for one who lies so near her heart?
And must she for the fatal loss bemoan,
Or faint to hear his last departing groan.

Me thinks I see him speechless gaze awhile,
And on her drop his last paternal smile;
With gushing tears closing his humid eyes,
The last pulse beats, and in her arms he dies.

With pallid cheeks she lingers round his bier,
And heaves a farewell sigh with every tear;

With sorrow she consigns him to the dust,
And silent owns the fatal sentence just.

Still her sequestered mother seems to weep,
And spurns the balm which constitutes her sleep;
Her plaintive murmurs float upon the gale,
And almost make the stubborn rocks bewail.

O what is like the awful breach of death,
Whose fatal stroke invades the creature's breath!
 It bids the voice of desolation roll,
And strikes the deepest awe within the bravest soul.

ON THE EVENING AND MORNING.

When Evening bids the Sun to rest retire,
Unwearied Ether sets her lamps on fire;
Lit by one torch, each is supplied in turn,
Till all the candles in the concave burn.

The night-hawk now, with his nocturnal tone,
Wakes up, and all the Owls begin to moan,
Or heave from dreary vales their dismal song,
Whilst in the air the meteors play along.

At length the silver queen begins to rise,
And spread her glowing mantle in the skies,
And from the smiling chambers of the east,
Invites the eye to her resplendent feast.

What joy is this unto the rustic swain,
Who from the mount surveys the moon-lit plain;
Who with the spirit of a dauntless *Pan*
Controls his fleecy train and leads the van;

Or pensive, muses on the water's side,
Which purling doth thro' green meanders glide,
With watchful care he broods his heart away
'Till night is swallowed in the flood of day.

The meteors cease to play, that mov'd so fleet
And spectres from the murky groves retreat,

The prowling wolf withdraws, which howl'd so bold
And bleating flocks may venture from the fold.

The night-hawk's din deserts the shepherd's ear.
Succeeded by the huntsman's trumpet clear,
O come Diana, start the morning chase
Thou ancient goddess of the hunting race.

Aurora's smiles adorn the mountain's brow,
The peasant hums delighted at his plough,
 And lo, the dairy maid salutes her bounteous cow.

ON THE POETIC MUSE.

Far, far above this world I soar,
And almost nature lose,
Aerial regions to explore,
With this ambitious Muse.

My towering thoughts with pinions rise,
Upon the gales of song,
Which waft me through the mental skies,
With music on my tongue.

My Muse is all on mystic fire,
Which kindles in my breast;
To scenes remote she doth aspire,
As never yet exprest.

Wrapt in the dust she scorns to lie,
Call'd by new charms away;
Nor will she e'er refuse to try
Such wonders to survey.

Such is the quiet bliss of soul,
When in some calm retreat,
Where pensive thoughts like streamlets roll,
And render silence sweet;

And when the vain tumultuous crowd
Shakes comfort from my mind,

My muse ascends above the cloud
And leaves the noise behind.

With vivid flight she mounts on high
Above the dusky maze,
And with a perspicacious eye
Doth far 'bove nature gaze.

CONSEQUENCES OF HAPPY MARRIAGES.

Hail happy pair, from whom such raptures rise,
On whom I gaze with pleasure and surprise;
From thy bright rays the gloom of strife is driven,
For all the smiles of mutual love are Heaven.

Thrice happy pair! no earthly joys excel
Thy peaceful state; there constant pleasures dwell,
Which cheer the mind and elevate the soul,
Whilst discord sinks beneath their soft control.

The blaze of zeal extends from breast to breast,
While Heaven supplies each innocent request;
And lo! what fond regard their smiles reveal,
Attractive as the magnet to the steel.

Their peaceful life is all content and ease,
They with delight each other strive to please;
Each other's charms, *they* only can admire,
Whose bosoms burn with pure connubial fire.

Th' indelible vestige of unblemished love,
Must hence a guide to generations prove:
Though virtuous partners moulder in the tomb,
Their light may shine on ages yet to come.

With grateful tears their well-spent day shall close,

When death, like evening, calls them to repose;
Then mystic smiles may break from deep disguise,
Like Vesper's torch transpiring in the skies.

Like constellations still their works may shine,
In virtue's unextinguished blaze divine;
Happy are they whose race shall end the same--
Sweeter than odours is a virtuous name.

Such is the transcript of unfading grace,
Reflecting lustre on a future race,
The virtuous on this line delight to tread,
And magnify the honors of the dead--

Who like a Phoenix did not burn in vain,
 Incinerated to revive again;
From whose exalted urn young love shall rise,
Exulting from a funeral sacrifice.

LINES,

On hearing of the intention of a gentleman to purchase The Poet's freedom.

When on life's ocean first I spread my sail,
I then implored a mild auspicious gale;
And from the slippery strand I took my flight,
And sought the peaceful haven of delight.

Tyrannic storms arose upon my soul,
And dreadful did their mad'ning thunders roll;
The pensive muse was shaken from her sphere,
And hope, it vanish'd in the clouds of fear.

At length a golden sun broke through the gloom,
And from his smiles arose a sweet perfume--
A calm ensued, and birds began to sing,
And lo! the sacred muse resumed her wing.

With frantic joy she chaunted as she flew,
And kiss'd the clement hand that bore her through;
Her envious foes did from her sight retreat,
Or prostrate fall beneath her burning feet.

'Twas like a proselyte, allied to Heaven--
Or rising spirits' boast of sins forgiven,
Whose shout dissolves the adamant away,
Whose melting voice the stubborn rocks obey.

'Twas like the salutation of the dove,
Borne on the zephyr through some lonesome grove,
When Spring returns, and Winter's chill is past,
And vegetation smiles above the blast.

'Twas like the evening of a nuptial pair,
When love pervades the hour of sad despair--
'Twas like fair Helen's sweet return to Troy,
When every Grecian bosom swell'd with joy.

The silent harp which on the osiers hung,
Was then attuned, and manumission sung:
Away by hope the clouds of fear were driven,
And music breathed my gratitude to Heaven.

Hard was the race to reach the distant goal,
The needle oft was shaken from the pole;
In such distress who could forbear to weep?
Toss'd by the headlong billows of the deep!

The tantalizing beams which shone so plain,
Which turned my former pleasures into pain--
Which falsely promised all the joys of fame,
Gave way, and to a more substantial flame.

Some philanthropic souls as from afar,
With pity strove to break the slavish bar;
To whom my floods of gratitude shall roll,
And yield with pleasure to their soft control.

And sure of Providence this work begun--
He shod my feet this rugged race to run;
And in despite of all the swelling tide,
Along the dismal path will prove my guide.

Thus on the dusky verge of deep despair,
Eternal Providence was with me there;
When pleasure seemed to fade on life's gay dawn,
And the last beam of hope was almost gone.

TO THE GAD-FLY.

Majestic insect! from thy royal hum,
The flies retreat, or starve before they'll come;
The obedient plough-horse may, devoid of fear,
Perform his task with joy, when thou art near.

As at the Lion's dread alarming roar,
The inferior beasts will never wander more,
Lest unawares he should be seized away,
And to the prowling monster fall a prey.

With silent pleasure often do I trace
The fly upon the wing, with rapid pace,
The fugitive proclaims upon the wind,
The death-bound sheriff is not far behind.

Ye thirsty flies beware, nor dare approach,
Nor on the toiling animal encroach;
Be vigilant, before you buzz too late,
The victim of a melancholy fate.

Such seems the caution of the once chased fly,
Whilst to the horse she dare not venture nigh;
This useful Gad-Fly traversing the field,
With care the lab'ring animal to shield.

Such is the eye of Providential care,
Along the path of life forever there;

Whose guardian hand by day doth mortals keep
And gently lays them down at night to sleep.

Immortal Guard, shall I thy pleasures grieve
Like Noah's dove, wilt thou the creature leave;
No never, never, whilst on earth I stay,
And after death, then fly with me away.

THE LOSS OF FEMALE CHARACTER.

See that fallen Princess! her splendor is gone--
The pomp of her morning is over;
 Her day-star of pleasure refuses to dawn,
 She wanders a nocturnal rover.

Alas! she resembles Jerusalem's fall,
The fate of that wonderful city;
When grief with astonishment rung from the wall,
 Instead of the heart cheering ditty.

When music was silent, no more to be rung,
When Sion wept over her daughter;
On grief's drooping willow their harps they were hung,
When pendent o'er Babylon's water.

She looks like some Star that has fall'n from her sphere,
No more by her cluster surrounded;
Her comrades of pleasure refuse her to cheer,
And leave her dethron'd and confounded.

She looks like some Queen who has boasted in vain,
Whose diamond refuses to glitter;
Deserted by those who once bow'd in her train,
Whose flight to her soul must be bitter.

She looks like the twilight, her sun sunk away,
He sets; but to rise again never!

Like the Eve, with a blush bids farewell to the day,
And darkness conceals her forever.

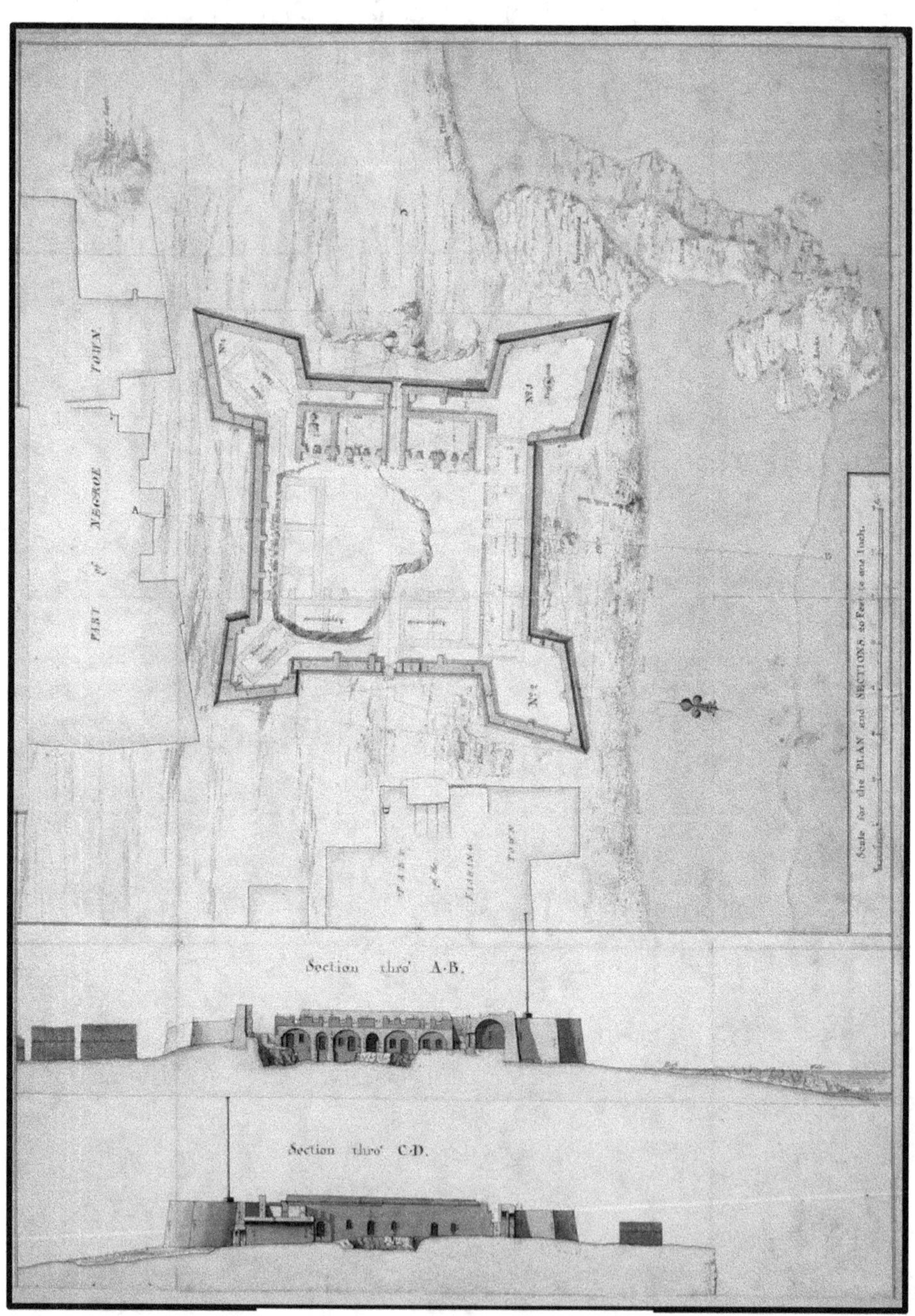

Annamaboe Fort, Ghana

PREPARED FOR PUBLICATION BY:
HISTORIC PUBLISHING

Slavery Books & African American History Resources
https://slaverybooks.blogspot.com

HISTORIC PUBLISHING
©2017
ALL RIGHTS RESERVED
WWW.HISTORICPUBLISHING.COM